*Love,
Deanna
Williams*

To..

This book is very special
It's been given to you with love
All the angels and the fairies
Will be watching from above

So when you start to read
This 'Pick-a-Woo Woo' book
We ask that you listen carefully
And at the pictures really look

Listen to your inner voice
Look at what is in your mind
Some very special messages
Will come your way you'll find

Please share your storybook
Enjoy it and have some fun
Please pass the loving messages
On to each and everyone

From..

To my Lexi…
I know where you hide your wings.

Miss Will Be is the future...
the next second, tomorrow, next year.

Mr. Now is this very second.

This is Miss Nina Lightning Bug.
a.k.a. "Miss N. Lightning"
She is Mr. Now's best friend.

Mr. Was Once is the Past...
a second ago, yesterday, last year.

Mr. Now closed his eyes and wished he was free.
"I bet you don't know how it feels being me.
No, it's not my birthday," grumbled Mr. Now.
"But I'm making a wish for myself anyhow."

"I'm not in the front and I'm not in the rear.
I'm bored and bogged down forever right here."
Mr. Now had grown incredibly dreary,
And waiting for happiness made him feel weary.

"I just know I'll be happy in some other time,
Or some other place would be simply sublime.
I'll wait right here for my tick-tock to chime,
To whisk me away to a yum-yummier time."

So he wished and waited and waited some more.
He waited so long that his footsies got sore.
After making his wish, he opened his eyes.
He was still where he was. A hum-drum surprise.

And with a KAPOW! Mr. Was Once did appear,
Clanged on his gong and said majestically clear:

"A Was Once can say with a chi-chi-la-chow,
Be sunny, my friend. Why, you are The Now."

"For I Was Once you, and you used to be ME...

Mind boggling, for sure, but you think cleverly."

Mr. Was Once announced, "MR. NOW, you're true-blue. The past and the future are sprouting from YOU!"

"Feeling stuck is a choice. I'm not sure you agree. Just open your cage and set yourself free!"

"Cheery hats you wish for, but it's important to see...

"Wow! So many hats!"

MR. NOW

MR. WAS-ONCE

They are always in grasp, if you choose them to be!"

"You're important, I say," and he boomed on his gong.
"To wear a hum-drum hat is amazingly wrong!"

You may have noticed, Mr. Now has a friend.
She shines super bright from her head to her end.

"Hello and Good Day with a buzzy-bugg-bee,
I'm Miss N. Lightning, how happy to see!
Mr. Now's my best friend, a trusty true pal,
I want him to be cheery right here in The Now."

"I'm Miss Nina Lightning Bug."

"He's so very important, as you will soon see,
A timely inventor of moments that be:
Yesterday and Tomorrow,
Last Week's on the list.
Yet, Mr. Now's the one moment which really exists...

Was Once's,
        Will Be's,
                Once Upon a Time's,

He invented **The End's** of all stories and rhymes."

Miss N. Lightning says in her very wise voice,
"From moment to moment you're making a choice.
When choosing a door read the sign up above:
You can never go wrong with faith, hope, and love."

"Mr. Now has a friend who he hasn't met yet.
She's arrived from the future to mend his mindset.
For what he decides, NOW, is important for sure.
You will find her hiding above the third door."

And as quick as a SNAP! Miss Will Be did appear.

She wiggled her wings and exclaimed with good cheer:

"A Will Be can say with a loo-loo-zen-dow:
'I know what it's like to be pals with The Now.'
For you Will Be me and I Was Once you,
And the choices we make Will Be future too-doo.

Miss Will Be proclaimed as she flooted her flute:

"All you are given is this moment...

This **ONE** **COLOSSAL**, teensy, *GLORIOUS*, Occasionally Tedious, *Yet Beautiful,* Silent, SCREAMING MOMENT!"

Wise choices are great,
simply choose from your heart.
Pick the best that you can.
We know that you're smart.

And last but not least
of the choices you live,
it's so very important
to choose to forgive.

Miss N. Lightning says, "If you want sunny days,
You'll have to make changes in some of your ways:
Let go of the past and give The Now wings,
Then see what the future so excitingly brings."

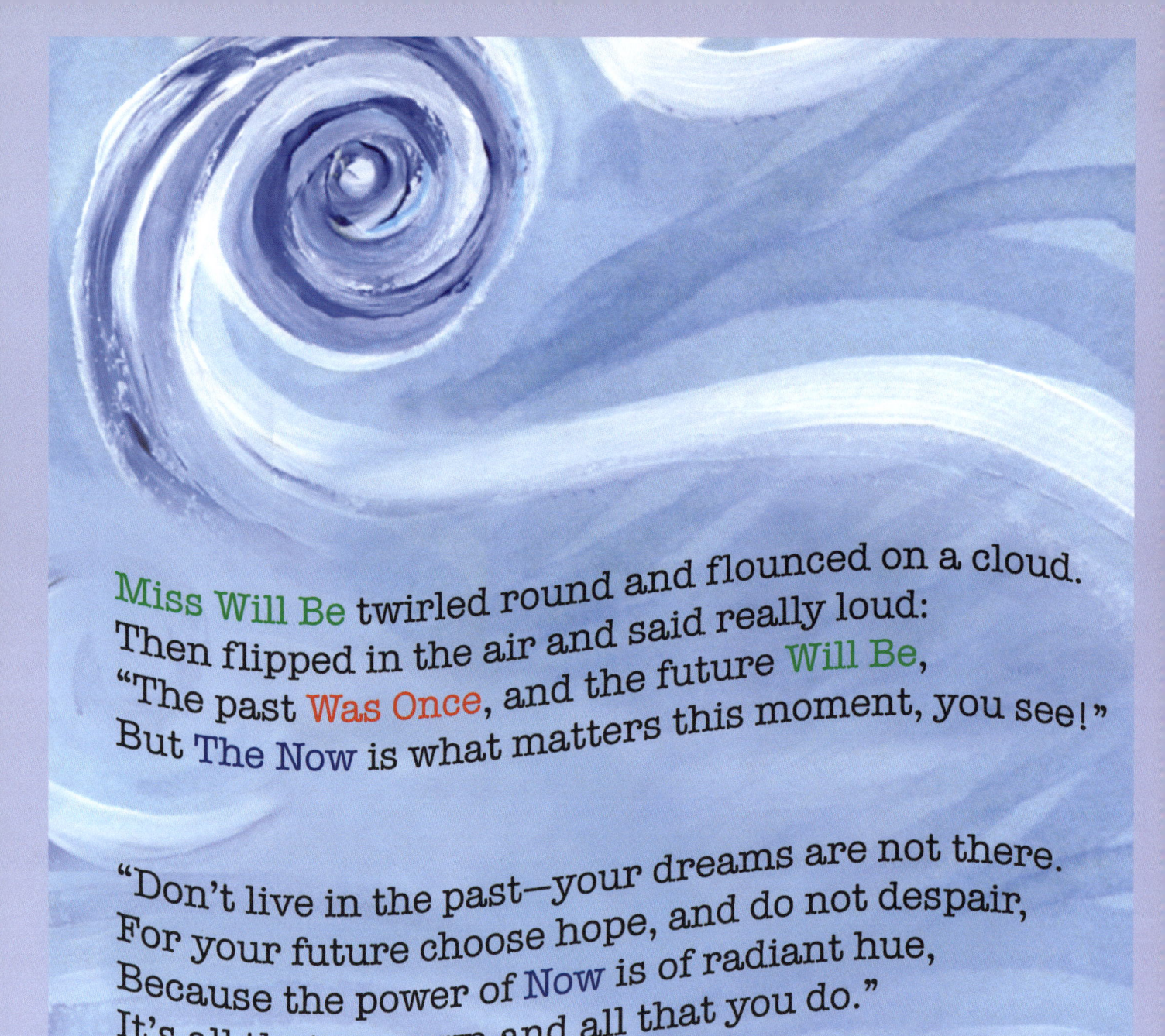

Miss Will Be twirled round and flounced on a cloud.
Then flipped in the air and said really loud:
"The past Was Once, and the future Will Be,
But The Now is what matters this moment, you see!"

"Don't live in the past—your dreams are not there.
For your future choose hope, and do not despair,
Because the power of Now is of radiant hue,
It's all that you own and all that you do."

Mr. Now became brilliant
And sparkled inside.
He sprang in the air
Feeling quite satisfied.
He grinned and he laughed,
And he burped really loud:
Out came his fear!
He was light as a cloud.

"When I am The Now, I'm spectacularly splendid.
All thought of what Was Once and Will Be is ended.
When I live as The Now and just simply be me,
I finally know what it's like to be free!"

"I'm in the music you make and the doors that you choose,
Cakes that you bake, even games you may lose."

"I'm less than a second, and more than a smile.
Be present this moment and you'll have stellar style."

"Each moment is special, it's perfectly true:

Know that this moment is waiting for you."

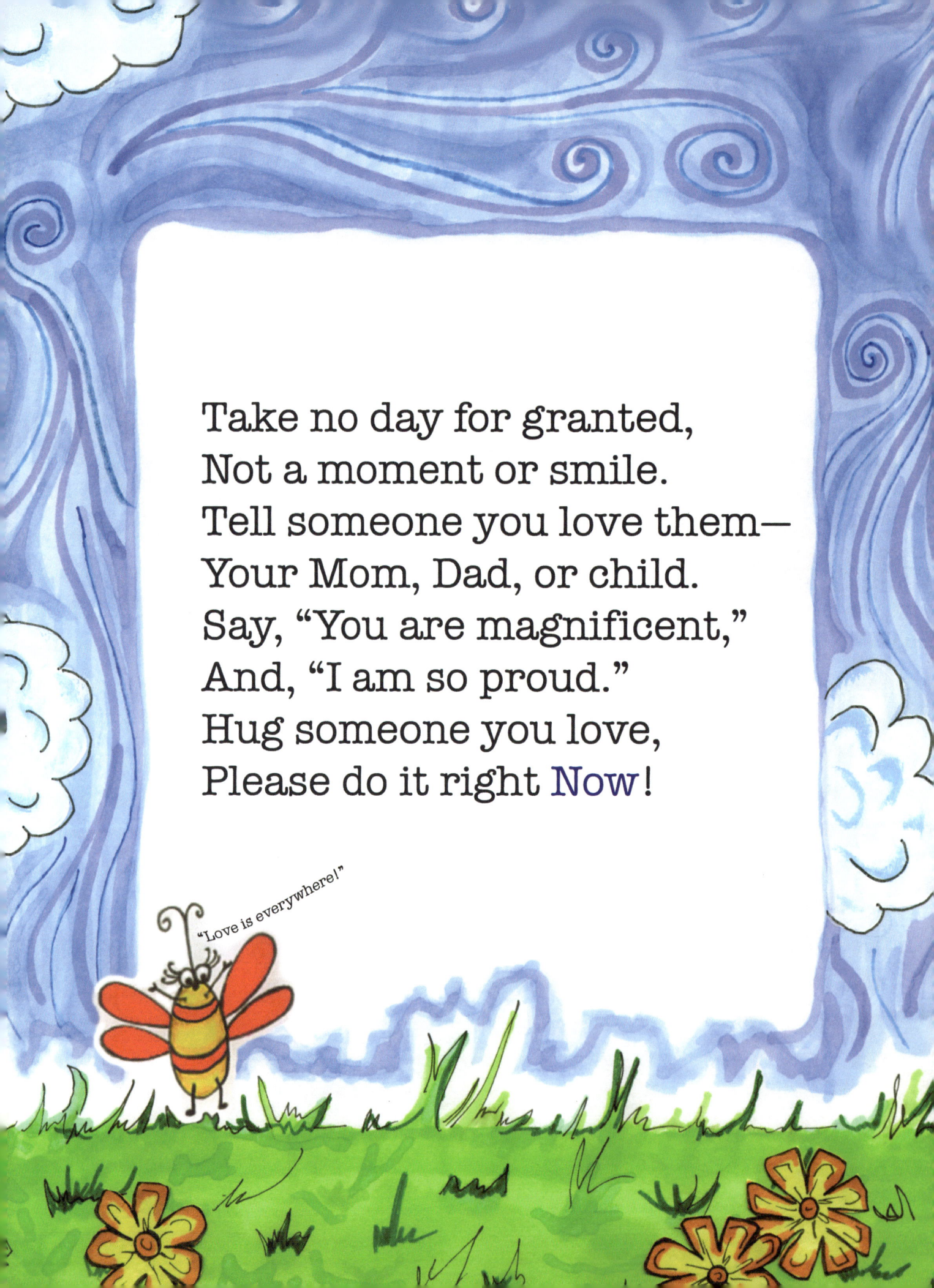

Take no day for granted,
Not a moment or smile.
Tell someone you love them—
Your Mom, Dad, or child.
Say, "You are magnificent,"
And, "I am so proud."
Hug someone you love,
Please do it right Now!

"Love is everywhere!"

Mr Now Meditation

For Parents:
To live in the present moment is actually quite simple. To believe otherwise is what is complicated. However, you can only live NOW. It is in this instant that you can remember your wholeness. You are not broken. You are whole. This can only be remembered in the present moment. The following meditation will help you to impart this knowledge to your children.

Meditation for Children (and big kids at heart):
ALL thoughts are your choice. You can deliberately think of any ideas you want. This is imagination.

Think of a purple parrot wearing a pickle on his head? Think of a blue cat with yellow polka dots. Think of your family giving you a big hug because they love you. Now imagine some ideas of your own. They can be simple ideas, or full of creativity. See? You CAN change your thoughts easily.

Now let us try out some more of your imagination...
Your true power only lies within you. Place your hands over where your heart lives.

Breathe. Within your mind, symbols of beauty appear. Waterfalls are glistening. Colorful flowers are blooming. A bright light is shining everywhere, surrounding all of your imaginings.

You begin running. First, you are running at a peaceful pace through mountain trails. You can hear the creek's water flowing gently over stones.

You can feel the air brush your face. It is cool and tickles your nose.

Soon you begin to run faster. Then faster... Soon you are running so fast that you lift off the ground. You are flying.

You have felt this feeling before, but you have forgotten. Now you remember. You look down and see your home. You fly over your school. It looks so tiny, as you are very high now. There are no worries about school. All of your teachers are trying to help you become your most creative self. You can touch the clouds. You do not feel alone, but you feel as if you are a part of everything. You realize that you can never be lonely. You see others flying, too. Some are flying above the clouds. All worries leave your mind, as only this moment exists. It is where peace lives, and this moment will never leave you. It is your friend.

Focus only on this moment...no thought of the past...no worry of future.

Just now. Feeling free to be as you are. Connected to the Source of Life.

Life IS, and will always be. Now...You are truly free.

Meet the Author - Deanna Williams

Deanna Williams is a visual artist, licensed massage therapist and dance instructor. Her main passion is teaching dance and art to children. She owned a dance studio in North Myrtle Beach, SC, for many years and currently teaches private art classes. She loves to paint fairies, angels, and magical beings. She even saw a fairy once! She lives near Nashville, Tennessee, USA, with her wonderful family and cutie-pie pets. She is also a columnist and radio co-host for The Faeries and Angels Magazine.

You can visit Deanna at www.artsydeanna.com.

"Love is everywhere!"

Pick-a-Woo Woo

Copyright 2011

The right of Deanna C. Williams to be identified as the Author and the Artist of the work has been asserted by her in accordance with the Copyright, Designs and Patents Act 1988.

All rights reserved. No part of this book may be used or reproduced, stored in a retrieval system, or transmitted in any form, or by any means electronic, mechanical, recording, photocopying, or in any manner whatsoever without permission in writing from the publisher, except for book reviews.

National Library of Australia Cataloguing-in-Publication entry
Author: Williams, Deanna C.
Title: Pick-a-WooWoo : Mr Now's magnificent moment : a tale about making every moment matter / Deanna C. Williams.
9781921883002 (pbk.)
Series: Pick-a-WooWoo children's book series ; 17.
Target Audience: For primary school children

Pick-a-WooWoo : Mr Now's Magnificent Moment
A tale about making every moment matter

With vivacious illustrations, wonderful humour and easy to read rhyming verse, this whimsical character, Mr Now, shows us that 'The present is a present, a gift just for you. You are special right now!'

"Here's a wonderful aspect of this children's book: it's done in such a way that every adult ought to have a copy too, because it really makes you realize how silly we are when we seek to escape the now instead of grasping the wonder of the moment." David Robert Ord, author of Your Forgotten Self.

Pick-a-Woo Woo

Published in Australia
• Pick-A-Woo Woo Publishers - www.pickawoowoo.com

Printed
• Lightning Source (US / UK / EUR)
• APOL Australasia Pty Ltd (AUS)

Distributed
• Brumby Books and Music (AUS)
• Ingram Book Group, Baker & Taylor, Barnes & Noble (UK/US/EUR)
• Amazon.com and other

Layout - www.masterpagedesign.co.uk

Most Pick-a-Woo Woo books can be found in good bookstores. If you are unable to order any of the Pick-a-Woo Woo Publishers children's books from your local bookseller, then please contact us at info@pickawoowoo.com or visit www.pickawoowoo.com and we will locate an outlet for you.

Pick-a-Woo Woo Divine Children's Books

Embrace Love, Touch the Heart, Kindle the Spirit and Enlighten the Mind.

The Pick-a-Woo Woo books for children are a series of books designed to encourage spiritual growth. Our books inspire joy and laughter and help create a more enlightened world by helping children with their mind, body, spirit connection.

Youngest Readers
Read Together 3-6 / Read Alone 5-6 years

Pick-a-Woo Woo: A Child Called Indigo — ISBN 978-0-9803669-8-3
Follow your heart, you are unique!

Pick-a-Woo Woo: The Little Sparkle In Me — ISBN 978-0-9806520-8-6
My sparkle is a gift to feel hear and see.

Pick-a-Woo Woo: Angel Steps — ISBN 978-0-9803669-9-0
Love You, Miss You.

Young Readers
Read Together 4-9 / Read Alone 6-9 years

Pick-a-Woo Woo: Wizards Words of Wisdom — ISBN 978-0-9803669-6-9
'Egone Missing' the ancient wizard shares his amazing secrets with you.

Pick-a-Woo Woo: Bliss — ISBN 978-0-9803669-4-5
A breathtaking story of transformation that reveals 'we are never alone.'

Pick-a-Woo Woo: The Happy Little Spirit — ISBN 978-0-9803669-1-4
Each of us has a Spirit but what is it and where did it come from?

Pick-a-Woo Woo: My Angel's Advice — ISBN 978-0-9803669-2-1
A Story about Love.

Pick-a-Woo Woo: Grandma's Great Advice — ISBN 978-0-9803669-3-8
The Art of Listening.

Pick-a-Woo Woo: Yep, I See Spirit — ISBN 978-0-9803669-5-2
The Gift of Sight.

Pick-a-Woo Woo: Frolicking with the Fairies — ISBN 978-0-9803669-0-7
Two Enchanting Fairytales.

Pick-a-Woo Woo: Born To Love Frogs — ISBN 978-0-9803669-7-6
All children have a gift!

Pick-a-Woo Woo: Oceans Calling — ISBN 978-0-9806520-1-7
An enlightening journey to the lost city of Atlantis.

Pick-a-Woo Woo: Mary Walks With Love — ISBN 978-0-9806520-9-3
Love Love Love!

Pick-a-Woo Woo: Angel Archie To The Rescue — ISBN 978-0-9806520-5-5
We can help the Earth too!

Older Readers
Read Together 5-11 / Read Alone 7-11 years

Pick-a-Woo Woo: KC the Conscious Camel — ISBN 978-0-9806520-3-1
A furry jaunt to peace and contentment.

Pick-a-Woo Woo: Robbie the Butterfly — ISBN 978-0-9806520-2-4
An enlightening story of transformation!

And more series, novels, picture books, e-books available (some are free).

Available at your local bookstore or visit www.pickawoowoo.com

LaVergne, TN USA
31 January 2011
214628LV00002B